I0055992

A Programmer's Guide to Computer Science Volume II

William M. Springer II, PhD

A Programmer's Guide to Computer Science, Volume II

By William M. Springer II

Published by Jaxson Media, Madison, WI, United States of America

© 2020 William M. Springer II

All rights reserved. No portion of this book may be reproduced in any form without permission from the publisher, except as permitted by U.S. copyright law.

Visit the author's website at `http://www.whatwill iamsaid.com/books/`.

ISBNs:

978-1-951204-04-4 (paperback)

978-1-951204-05-1 (hardcover)

978-1-951204-06-8 (ebook)

Library of Congress Control Number: 2019909527

First Edition, First Printing, 2020

Cover design and images without source cited by Brit Springer at Moonlight Designs Studio - `https://moonli ghtdesignsstudio.com/`. Typesetting done by the author in LaTeX. Technical editing by Nicholas R Allgood. Copy editing by Margo Simon.

Contents

Introduction

Why this book?

When I originally started sending the rough draft of A Programmer's Guide to Computer Science out for review, I consistently got the same feedback. Too much material. Too much to process. Too intimidating.

That feedback led to several changes. The text was shortened and simplified; details that wouldn't be immediately relevant were removed. The book was broken up so that Volume I contained only the most important topics. The result was a less intimidating, more readable book.

Volume II follows the same easy-to-read style as Volume I, but covers more specialized content. The topics in this volume are less likely to come up in a job interview. They still, however, form part of a well-rounded computer science education and aid in writing better code.

Overview

The various sections of this volume are fairly independent and can be read in any order. They intentionally scratch the surface of a variety of areas.

The final section, Advanced Topics, covers the more esoteric subjects referenced in earlier chapters.

What comes next?

In both volumes of this series, I have been deliberately concise, leaving out details that, while interesting, are not important for understanding the underlying concepts. In future books, I hope to go more in-depth into some areas of particular interest.

To suggest a topic you'd like to see in a future volume, sign up for the mailing list, or just ask a question, visit my website at `http://www.whatwilliamsaid.com/books/`. I look forward to hearing from you.

Part VIII

Proofs

Chapter 17

Acceptable Proofs

17.1   Intro to proofs

The wonderful thing about mathematics is that we can create proofs that will hold up indefinitely. If the axioms[1] are correct and the chain of logic that links those axioms to the given result is correct, then the result will always hold.

A valid proof must demonstrate that a statement is always true. It is never sufficient to demonstrate that the statement holds in a great many cases; every case must be covered.

> **Example**
> A pair of twin primes is two prime numbers

---

[1]An axiom is a statement that is accepted as true; additional statements are then shown to follow logically from the axiom. Euclid, for example, had as one of his axioms that any two points may be connected by a straight line.

that are two apart (e.g., 5 and 7, 11 and 13, 17 and 19.). The twin prime conjecture[a] states that there are infinitely many twin primes. This seems reasonable, as we know there are an infinite number of primes[b], but not obvious, since primes don't follow any known pattern.

At the time of this writing, the largest known twin primes, $2996863034895 * 2^{1290000}$ plus or minus 1, are 388,342 digits long. The great number of twin primes found strongly suggests that they will continue forever - but isn't a proof!

---

[a]A conjecture is something we think is true but don't know how to prove.
[b]Euclid's second theorem.

A phrase that is often employed (but should never be used) by students is "it is obvious" or "it is easy to show". A proper mathematical proof does not skip steps. A textbook may omit simple steps for brevity, but a proof requires that the full chain of logic remain intact.

17.2 Nomenclature

Axiom
    A statement that is accepted without proof; the rest of the proof depends on the correctness of the axioms.

Conjecture
    Something that is suspected to be true but has not yet been proven. When a conjecture is proven, it

becomes a theorem.[2]

Corollary
>A statement that immediately follows from another theorem or definition. Often this is simply a restriction of the theorem to some special case.

Hypothesis
>A conjecture that is assumed to be true, although it has not been proven. Sometimes a hypothesis will be taken as true and used to develop conditional proofs of other conjectures.

Lemma
>A minor result that is proved as part of a proof of a larger theorem. If the desired proof is the peak of Mt. Everest, a lemma is a stop along the climb; proving it hopefully gets you that much closer to where you want to be.[3]

Proof
>A mathematical proof is a series of logical steps which show the conclusion is guaranteed from the stated assumptions. Often the abbreviation QED[4] or a square is used to denote the end of the proof.

---

[2]If disproved, it is simply a false conjecture.

[3]For example, Euclid's lemma says that if a prime p divides the product ab of two integers a and b, then it must divide at least one of those two integers. This simple lemma is used in proving the fundamental theorem of arithmetic, which states that every integer greater than one either is prime or has a unique (up to ordering) prime factorization.

[4]"Quod Erat Demonstrandum", Latin for "what was to be shown," meaning, I have proved what I set out to prove.

Theorem
A statement that has been proven to be true using axioms and/or previously proven theorems. When a conjecture is proven, it becomes a theorem.

Chapter 18

Proof Techniques

18.1 Proof by construction, proof by exhaustion

Proof by construction and proof by exhaustion are often confused.[1]

In a proof by construction, we prove that a particular object exists by constructing an example of such an object. If my conjecture is that there exist two primes with a difference of two, I can prove the conjecture by providing a pair of such primes (for example, 17 and 19). The goal is simply to show that the desired object exists, so one such object is sufficient.

In a proof by exhaustion,[2] we break the problem down

---

[1]Students misusing proof by construction often leads the professor to exhaustion.

[2]This is also called proof by cases, because we break down the problem into a finite number of cases (each of which could potentially contain an infinite number of examples) and prove all of them.

into some number of cases and prove each one separately. The pumping lemma, discussed in Chapter 13, is a proof by exhaustion: we take a string that belongs to the language and show that any machine generating that string will also generate strings which are not in the language.

Example

The four-color theorem[a] states that no planar graph requires more than four colors. Appel and Haken proved the theorem exhaustively by demonstrating that a minimal counterexample must contain one of 1,936 possible configurations, each of which was checked by computer.

[a]See Section 4.7 on Graph Coloring.

18.2   Proof by contradiction

In proof by contradiction, we assume that the statement we wish to disprove is actually true and show that this leads to a logical contradiction - something that cannot also be true.

Example

An irrational number is a real number that cannot be written as the ratio of two integers.

Suppose we wish to prove that $\sqrt{2}$ is irrational. Assume it's actually rational; then $\sqrt{2} = a/b$ for some smallest integers a and b. Rearranging, we get $b\sqrt{2}=a$. Squaring both sides, we get $b^2 * 2 = a^2$.

Since a^2 is twice b^2, a must be even, so we can set it equal to double a third number: $a = 2c$. So now we have $2b^2 = (2c)^2 = 4c^2$. Now $b=2c^2$, so b is even, contradicting the assumption that a and b were the smallest integers whose quotient is $\sqrt{2}$.[a] Therefore our initial assumption was false, and $\sqrt{2}$ is not a rational number.

[a] If a and b were the smallest such integers, they could not have a common factor.

When we would like to do proof by construction but do not know how to actually construct the object, an alternative is to show that the non-existence of the object would result in a contradiction. A proof that demonstrates that an object must exist without actually constructing it is known as a non-constructive proof.

18.3   Proof by induction

A proof by induction has two steps. First, we prove one or more base cases. Here we show that for the smallest cases we're interested in, the hypothesis is true.

Then we prove an inductive step, showing that if the statement holds for size k, it also holds for size $k+1$. We have multiple base cases when this step depends on more than one previous step, or if the proof requires that the previous step be of some minimal size larger than the smallest case we wish to prove.

This gives us the following train of logic. The conjecture is true for case one. Because it's true for case one, it must be true for case two. Because it's true for case two, it must be true for case three. Because it's true for case n, it must be true for case $n{+}1$. Once we've shown that the base case is true and that every case implies the next largest case, we know we can extend that to any n and the theorem is proven.

18.3.1 Example

Imagine that we have a chessboard with one square removed, For example, such a 2 x 2 chessboard would like look this:

We can call this shape an L. Now imagine that we have a 2^n x 2^n chessboard with one square removed. We wish to prove that it can be tiled (that is, every square that has not been removed is covered and nothing else is covered) with only L-shaped pieces.

Our base case is the 2 x 2 board with one square removed that we saw above. By definition, this board is just an L, so clearly it can be tiled.

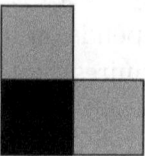

Suppose that the statement holds true for a board of size up to 2^k x 2^k; this is our *inductive hypothesis* (IH). Consider a board of size 2^{k+1} x 2^{k+1}. This is the same as having a 2 x 2 grid of 2^k x 2^k boards.

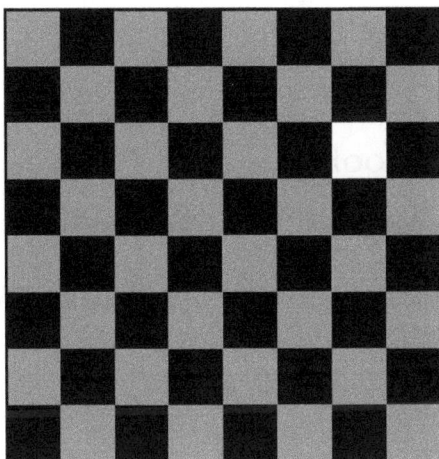

Lay a tile so that it has one square on each of the three quarters that are not already missing a square. We now have four 2^k x 2^k boards, each with one square missing (or covered), which by the inductive hypothesis can be tiled.

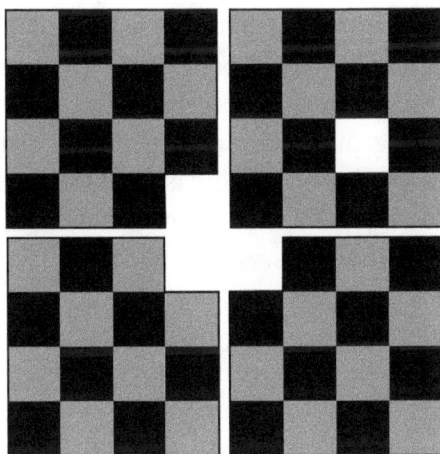

This is a tiling of the entire 2^{k+1} x 2^{k+1} chessboard, which proves that any such board can be tiled for any positive integer k.

18.3.2 Faulty proof

Suppose I want to prove that all horses are the same color.[3]

Base case: Suppose I have one horse. It is clearly the same color as itself.

Inductive hypothesis: For any set of horses of up to size k, all of them are the same color.

Inductive step: Suppose we have $k+1$ horses. By the IH, the first k of them are the same color. By the IH, the last k of them are the same color. Since these two groups overlap, all of the horses in the group have the same color; therefore, every horse has the same color!

What went wrong? In this example we actually needed two base cases. The inductive step assumed that the first and last k horses in the group overlap, which isn't true if $k=1$. We needed to also show a base case of two horses, but we're not able to show that two horses must be the same color and so the proof fails.

---

[3]This is not actually true.

18.4 Proof by contrapositive

Often when trying to prove a statement, it is easier to prove a modified (possibly stronger) version of the statement that then implies what we actually wanted to prove. In proof by contrapositive, we take advantage of the fact that if A implies B ($A \implies B$), it logically follows that not B implies not A ($\overline{B} \implies \overline{A}$). If the contrapositive is true, the original statement must also be true or we would have both A and $\overline{A}$.

Example

Suppose we want to prove that if k is an irrational number, $\sqrt{k}$ must also be an irrational number.

The contrapositive of this is that if $\sqrt{k}$ is a rational number, k must also be a rational number.

Suppose $\sqrt{k}$ is rational; then it is the ratio of two integers: $\sqrt{k} = a \,/\, b$.

Squaring both sides, we get $k = a^2/b^2$. This equation shows that k is also the ratio of two integers and thus is rational.

This chain of reasoning proves that if $\sqrt{k}$ is rational, then k must also be rational, and by contrapositive, if k is irrational, then $\sqrt{k}$ must also be irrational.

Chapter 19

Certificates

Suppose we have a previously-proven algorithm that solves a given problem. If we then implement that algorithm in a program, can we be certain that the program gives the correct solution?

> Beware of bugs in the above code; I have only proved it correct, not tried it.
>
> - Donald Knuth[1]

The difficulty is that while the algorithm may be correct, we can't be sure that the implementation of that algorithm doesn't contain errors. We would like to have a way to check that the program is actually returning the correct answer.

A proof of correctness is known as a certificate; something we can easily check to show that the answer is correct. For example, consider a program which determines

---

[1]D. E. Knuth, *Notes on the van Emde Boas construction of priority deques: An instructive use of recursion*, classroom notes, March 1977

whether or not a number is prime. If the answer is no, a certificate would be a set of integers whose product is the number we are testing.

Our goal is that checking a certificate will be faster and simpler (have a lower asymptotic runtime and less complexity) than the original problem, so that we can be more certain the program verifying the certificate does not contain errors. We say that a certificate is strong if the verification algorithm has a better time bound than the original problem, and weak if it does not; in practice, algorithms often have a strong rejection certificate and a weak acceptance certificate, or vice versa.[2]

---

[2]D. Kratsch, R.M. McConnell, K. Mehlhorn, J.P. Spinrad, *Certifying algorithms for recognizing interval graphs and permutation graphs*, ACM-SIAM SODA, 14 (2003), 866-875.

Example

Checking whether a graph is bipartite takes $O(n+m)$ time. If it is bipartite, an acceptance certificate is a two-coloring of the graph, which also requires $O(n+m)$ time to verify, making it a weak certificate. If it is not, a rejection certificate (an odd cycle) can be verified in $O(n)$ time and thus is a strong certificate.

Part IX

Security and Privacy

Chapter 20

Intro to Security

Loosely speaking, security is anything involved in keeping people from doing things they are not allowed to do. We can break these down into violations of confidentiality, integrity, and availability.

20.1 Confidentiality

Consider the following information:

- A conversation between a patient and her doctor in a medical portal

- A spreadsheet containing advertising spend for a political campaign

- A list of user logins and passwords for popular shopping websites

In each case, it is important that the information

remains confidential.[1] A violation of confidentiality exposes information to someone not authorized to have it. Possible causes include:

- A company does not have a policy prohibiting the release of information, or employees did not follow that policy. For example, a website that stores confidential documents in a location where they can be accessed by a web crawler.[2]

- A malicious user gained access by masquerading as a trusted user (a failure of authentication). The legitimate user may click on an email purporting to be from Amazon, end up on a spoof site, and enter his login credentials; the attacker can now go on a shopping spree.

- A malicious user is able to read a file that should have been unreadable (a failure of encryption). The file may be encrypted using an obsolete encryption scheme or easy-to-guess password.

- A malicious user is able to intercept data while it is being transmitted between authorized users.

Storing and transmitting information securely often requires encryption, which we'll discuss in the next two chapters.

---

[1]Sometimes even the existence of the information needs to remain confidential. For example, the fact that a patient is communicating with an oncologist reveals private medical information.

[2]Don't laugh. I've accidentally run across complete tax returns while searching for completely unrelated things.

20.2　Integrity

Integrity refers to the trustworthiness of the data, and encompasses two areas: data integrity (whether the information is correct) and origin integrity (whether we know where the information came from).

We need to ensure that the data is accurate, which means having mechanisms in place to prevent unauthorized changes or detect when an unauthorized change occurs.[3] We also want to know where the data comes from, as this reflects on its trustworthiness: medical advice has a higher degree of credibility if it comes from a doctor rather than a receptionist. Integrity mechanisms can ensure both that we know who sent a message and that we can prove it; we discuss this more in Chapter 22.

20.3　Availability

If an attacker cannot compromise a system, he may still be able to make it unavailable for use. These attempts can range from simply trying to make a service unavailable to anyone (for example, launching a denial of service attack against a popular website) to causing delays that enable a second attack (causing a failover from a secure server to a compromised one).

20.4　Goals

The various security mechanisms have three goals:

---

[3]This change doesn't have to be malicious. A checksum can be used for detecting both deliberate alterations and random errors.

- Preventing an attack from being successful. A strong password policy is an attempt to protect a system from unauthorized users.

- Recovering from the attack. This could mean restoring a deleted or altered file from backup or taking legal action against the attacker.

- Detecting when an attack has occurred. This could mean detecting an attack in progress so that it can be prevented (for example, locking out a user after several incorrect login attempts) or simply identifying a past intrusion and implementing recovery measures.

Chapter 21

Intro to Cryptography

Cryptography is the study and practice of secure communication, and covers a wide array of mathematical techniques[1]. It could be considered one of the most dangerous branches of computer science due to the frequency of poor execution and the possible consequences of an insecure cryptographical system.

Avoiding having a message intercepted can be done in a number of ways. The simplest (in concept if not in execution) is to simply hide the message; ideally the adversary will not even know that a message is being sent.

People have used *steganography* (the practice of concealing the existence of a message) for thousands of years. According to the Greek historian Herodotus, the tyrant Histiaeus shaved the head of a servant, had a message tattooed on his scalp, then sent him on (after his hair had grown back) with instructions to shave him again.

---

[1] For a more in-depth (but easy to read) history of cryptography, see *The Code Book* by Simon Singh.

In modern times, an image or other file may have another message hidden within it - often in plain sight. Where cryptography protects the contents of a message, steganography also protects the fact that a message is being sent.

A message can be encrypted in one of two ways, codes or ciphers. When using a cipher, letters (or groups of letters) are replaced with other letters (or groups of letters). For example, in the well-known Caesar cipher, each letter of the alphabet is replaced by the letter some number of positions further down.[2] In a code, words or phrases have a predetermined meaning that is not directly related to the text; for example, "chicken soup" could be taken to mean "attack at dawn."

21.1 Modern cryptography

In the past, secret-keeping largely relied on security through obscurity, which could have been in the form of hiding the message or relying on an adversary's lack of knowledge of how to decrypt an encrypted text.

Modern cryptography depends instead on mathematics. We prefer a cryptosystem designed so that if an adversary has a copy of the encrypted text (the *ciphertext*) and knows exactly how it was encrypted, he still cannot read the message without knowing the shared secret (that is, the *key*). Knowing the secret allows us to decrypt the message and recover the *plaintext*.

---

[2]Caesar himself is said to have used a shift of three letters when communicating with his generals.

21.2 Terminology

Traditionally, we have a message which is being sent from Alice to Bob. A third party, Eve, would like to eavesdrop on that message.

Alice and Bob have some information which allows them to communicate securely. If they are using a *symmetric* algorithm, then the key is a shared secret. Alice and Bob each have a copy of the key, which is used for both encryption and decryption. Symmetric key cryptography requires that the participants have a way to securely agree on a key before using it to transmit messages. This required key exchange is the primary disadvantage of symmetric algorithms, as it requires that two parties wishing to communicate arrange to meet in advance or find some already existing method of secure communication. This problem can be avoided using *quantum key distribution*, in which properties of quantum mechanics are used to distribute keys securely.

Asymmetric algorithms, often known as *public key* algorithms, use different keys for encryption and decryption. A message which is encrypted with the public key can be decrypted with the private key.

In some cases, the reverse is also true: the person with the private key can encrypt a message and anyone with the public key can decrypt it. In this case, the private key can be used for authentication: the owner of the key can sign a document and anyone with the public key can verify that signature.[3]

---

[3] However, this can weaken the security of the encryption scheme and is generally not recommended. Rather, the keyholder should have separate keys for decrypting and signing.

21.3 Perfectly secure communication

In theory, almost any cipher can be broken, given sufficient time and computing power. The greater the amount of ciphertext transmitted that uses the same key, the easier such decryption becomes. For example, when using a substitution cipher (in which each letter is replaced with another letter), as the length of a text increases, the letter frequency will tend towards the characteristic distribution for the language used, and it becomes more practical to decrypt the text using frequency analysis.

The exception - and the only encryption method that cannot be cracked through cryptographic techniques - is the one-time pad. In this case, Alice and Bob have a shared key which is at least as long as the text to be transmitted, and each letter of the text is combined with the corresponding letter of the pad to obtain the ciphertext. As long as the pad is truly random, kept secret, and never reused, the resulting ciphertext cannot be decrypted. The difficulty lies in generating and distributing these one-time pads (and this in fact is one of the problems solved by quantum cryptography).

21.4 Quantum key distribution

The best-known application of quantum cryptography is quantum key distribution, which allows Alice and Bob to generate a key without ever having to meet in person or have any other form of secure (private) communication.

It is required that Alice and Bob can also commu-

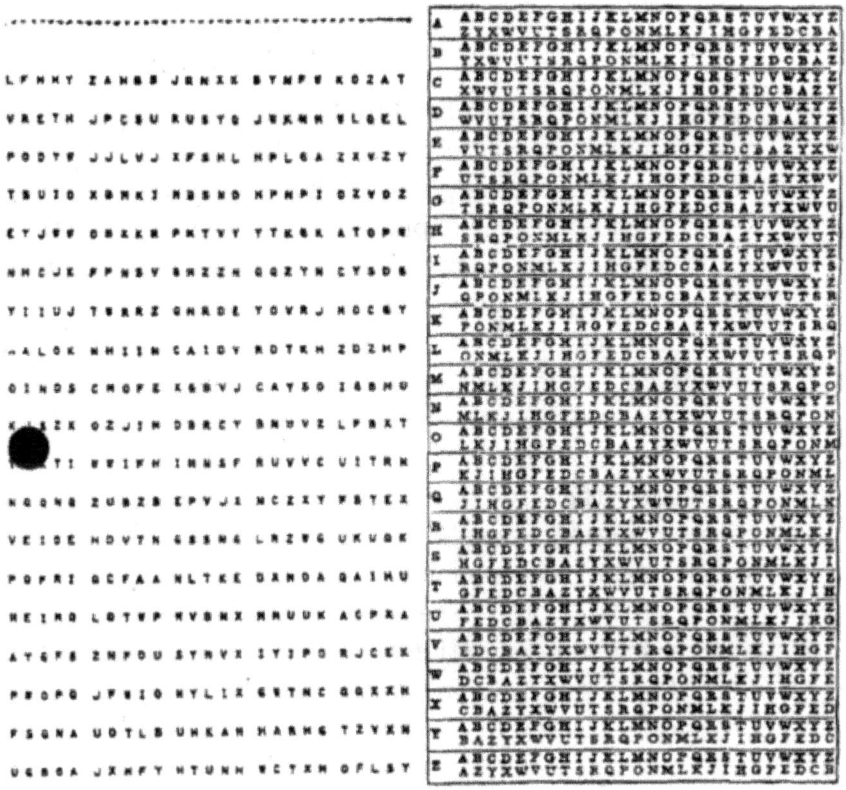

Figure 21.1: A one-time pad formerly used by the NSA. To the left is the pad itself; to the right are instructions for encrypting each letter of the plaintext given the corresponding letter of the pad. Declassified public domain image from https://www.governmentattic.org/18docs/Hist_US_COMSEC_Boak_NSA_1973u.pdf.

nicate over an authenticated classical channel - that is, they can send messages (not necessarily private) and be sure that they're talking to each other rather than to an impersonator.

Quantum key distribution depends on the fact that an eavesdropper would have to measure the message being sent (potentially altering it), and this can be detected.

The classic example uses photon polarization states. Alice sends a stream of photons and measures their states, but for each one she randomly chooses either a rectilinear or diagonal polarization. When Bob receives the photons, he does the same. They then compare the polarizations they chose for each photon (over the classical channel) and discard the ones that do not match.

They now choose a random subset of the photons and compare their results. If there is no eavesdropper and the quantum channel is sufficiently reliable, nearly all of the measurements should match. However, if Eve intercepted the photons, then any photon she measured with an incorrect polarization (which will, on average, be half of them) will have its orientation "scrambled" for the correct polarization. When Bob measures that photon, he receives a random orientation. As a result, his measurements will not match Alice's for approximately one quarter of the intercepted photos and they can conclude that the quantum channel is not secure.

Quantum key distribution systems have been commercially available for some time.

Chapter 22

Public Key Cryptography

In asymmetric cryptography, different keys are necessary to encrypt and decrypt the message. We use this type of encryption for public key cryptography, in which the encryption key is publicly distributed while the decryption key is kept private.

22.1 Using public and private keys

If Alice wants to send Bob a message, she first looks up his public key and uses that to encrypt the message. She can then send Bob the message, or even post it on an open forum. When Bob receives the message, he uses his private key to decrypt it. The key[1] to the system

---

[1]No pun intended (although I usually intend my puns).

working is that an attacker cannot (using known techniques) determine the private key from the public key **in a reasonable amount of time.**[2]

The use of private keys also allows Alice to authenticate that she is the one sending the message. After encrypting the message, Alice encrypts it again using her private key and attaches that copy as a signature. Anyone with her public key can decrypt the signature to verify that it matches the original encrypted message, which demonstrates that the sender knew Alice's private key.[3]

Asymmetric cryptography uses a one-way or trapdoor function. This is a mathematical function that is easy to compute in one direction, but (believed to be) difficult to compute in the other without some secret information.

> **The Math**
>
> Let f be a function such that $f(x) = y$. If f is a good trapdoor function, then computing y from x is easy, but computing x from y is impractical without the key.

---

[2]If something needs to be kept secret for a week and the cipher requires three years of effort to break, it is likely to be sufficiently secure.

[3]Signing the message in this way also provides non-repudiation. Alice cannot later claim that she did not send the message without also claiming that someone else knows her private key.

22.2   RSA

RSA[4] is one of the most commonly used algorithms for public key cryptography.

In the RSA algorithm, Alice chooses two large primes p and q of similar lengths and computes $n=pq$. This is a one-way function because multiplying two integers is easy, but factoring the result into its component primes is not.

22.2.1   Creating the keys

Alice uses her two large primes p and q and their product n to generate a public key e and a private key d, where d cannot be easily determined from e. She announces both e and n, so the encryption key e and the product n are publicly known.

22.2.2   Encrypting with the public key

When Bob wants to send Alice a message M, he converts M to an integer m to be encrypted. He then performs the following operations:

1. Bob raises m to the power of e: $m'=m^e$.

2. He takes the result mod n, to get the cipertext c: $c = m' \bmod n$.

---

[4]The initials stand for Ron Rivest, Adi Shamir, and Leonard Adleman, who first described the algorithm.

22.2.3 Decrypting with the private key

When Alice receives the message (c), she undoes the encryption using her private key.

1. First she raises the ciphertext to the power of d: $c' = c^d$.

2. She then takes the modulus to recover the original encrypted integer: $m = c' \bmod n$.

3. Finally, she converts m back to the message M, which she can now read.

The Math

Why does this work? Fermat's little theorem states that if p is a prime number and a is an integer, $a^p \equiv a \bmod p$. The symbol $\equiv$ means congruent; the two sides are equivalent with respect to the modulus. For example, 3 and 15 are congruent mod 12, which is why the third hour (3am) and 15th hour (3pm) are in the same position on a 12-hour clock.

In this case, the message m is being raised to the power of e and then to the power of d, mod n. Raising a value to one exponent and then to a second exponent is equivalent to raising the original value to the product of the two exponents, so after running both the encryption and decryption we have $m^{ed} \bmod n$. Alice chooses e and d such that this will leave us with m, the original message.

22.2.4 Attempts at interception

In order for Eve to decode the message, she needs to know d. To calculate d she needs to factor n into its prime components (thus re-creating the private key), which is difficult. Thus, the message is considered secure because Eve cannot (given current technology and mathematical techniques) break the encryption in a reasonable amount of time.

22.3 Performance considerations

In practice, because symmetric key cryptography is faster than asymmetric key cryptography, the asymmetric keys will be used to exchange symmetric keys known as session keys, which will then be used to encrypt and decrypt the actual data for the session. This method provides the convenience of asymmetric key cryptography, the speed of symmetric key cryptography, and the security of frequent key replacement (as each symmetric key will be used for only one session).

This is how SSL works. The browser gets a copy of the server's asymmetric key, then creates a session key, encrypts it, and sends it to the server. The server decrypts that message using its private key and then the shared secret is used to encrypt the rest of the session.

The reason symmetric key encryption is faster is that asymmetric encryption requires a larger key.[5] Because

---

[5]Symmetric key algorithms generally use keys between 128 and

a symmetric key can just be a random number, it has security equal to its key length. The asymmetric key is chosen using a known algorithm, so a given key space contains fewer distinct keys and those keys have patterns that an attacker can use. As a result, the key space for an asymmetric algorithm needs to be longer than that for a symmetric key algorithm to obtain a comparable level of security.

For example, in the RSA algorithm (explained above) the private key is composed of two prime numbers, so all non-primes can be ignored as they cannot possibly be part of the key.

---

256 bits, while asymmetric algorithms typically use keys between 1,024 and 4,096 bits.

Chapter 23

User Authentication

Passwords have been used to determine access for thousands of years. In the internet age, however, passwords often do not provide sufficient security, for several reasons.

Weak passwords - Given a system that allows unlimited password tries, an attacker can simply try every possible password until arriving at the correct one. This can be an exhaustive key search (trying literally every legal combination) or a dictionary attack (trying everything in a list of common passwords).

Reused passwords - Even a strong password can be discovered. If an attacker gains access to a password that is associated with the same username or email across multiple sites, the attacker now has access to each of those sites.

Adding length and complexity requirements for passwords helps mitigate the first problem, but increases the odds that the user will reuse the password (who wants to memorize multiple long, complicated passwords?), store it somewhere that an attacker could potentially access,[1] or risk forgetting it. Password managers (which only require that the user remember one master password while generating and storing a strong password for each website) are one solution, although they then represent a single point of attack to gain access to all of a user's accounts.[2]

Other options for increasing password security include:

Forced password change - Until recently, Microsoft recommended that companies force employees to change their passwords frequently, under the assumption that shared passwords might eventually leak. These frequent changes exacerbate the issues discussed above (users who are required to change passwords frequently tend to choose passwords that are easy to remember) and are no longer recommended.[3] Passwords that have not been stolen do not need to be changed, and passwords that you suspect have been stolen should be changed immediately.

Banned password lists - In addition to minimum length requirements, a user's password can be compared

---

[1]In 2018, a White House staffer made news when he wrote down his encrypted email passwords on a piece of White House stationary, which he left at a bus stop.

[2]In 2019, a caching bug in popular password manager LastPass allowed it to leak the last-used password to a malicious website.

[3]https://blogs.technet.microsoft.com/secguide/2019/05/23/security-baseline-final-for-windows-10-v1903-and-windows-server-v1903/

to a list of common passwords and disallowed if it
is found.

Password hashing - A secure website will not allow
you to retrieve a lost password, because it never actually saves the password. Instead, it combines the
password with a salt (a secret string, unique to each
user),[4] hashes the resulting value,[5] and saves the
hashed value. Thus, even if the password database
is compromised, the attacker still would still need
to individually crack each password.

Multi-factor authentication - There are three factors
commonly used for authentication: something you
know, something you have, and something you are.
Typical examples are a password for logging in to
a website, a smartcard for accessing a building at
work, and a fingerprint for unlocking a phone. Using a chip-and-PIN credit card requires two of these:
something you have (the card itself) and something
you know (the PIN).[6] Many websites are now offer-

---

[4]The reason the salt must be unique to each user is to prevent
the use of rainbow tables, which are reverse lookup tables which
store a password that hashes to each value. Given the database of
hashed passwords, we can look up a password (not necessarily the
original one) that hashes to the saved value for the desired account,
allowing access. Adding a salt which is unique to each user means
that the same hash table can no longer be used repeatedly, which
removes its value.

[5]For an introduction to hashing, see Section 2.5.

[6]As another example, entering Disney World on a multi-day
ticket requires using a fingerprint scanner, so depends on both
something you have (your ticket) and something you are (your
fingerprint).

ing two-factor authentication,[7] which require both your password and a second, temporary access code that shows you have access to a phone number or device associated with the account.

---

[7]Two-factor authentication, or 2FA, is a subset of multi-factor authentication in which exactly two of the factors are used.

Part X

Hardware and Software

Chapter 24

Hardware Abstractions

Most of us are not interested in writing machine code to directly control computer hardware. Instead, we use a set of abstractions that allow us to access resources of a particular type rather than memorize the physical details of a given resource. These abstractions can take place at multiple levels.

- When we make calls to the operating system, we only need to know the operating system's APIs rather than the specific instruction set of the CPU that operating system is running on.

- When writing in a high-level language, we can use generic commands that the compiler will translate into CPU-specific instructions.

24.1 Physical storage

Consider how data is physically stored, as a collection of zeroes and ones.

For a traditional hard disk drive, the bits are stored on circular platters divided into tracks (concentric circles) and sectors (pie-shaped wedges on a track). Each sector contains a number[1] of tiny areas, each of which is individually magnetized or demagnetized. As the platters spin, the read/write heads move into place above the appropriate areas and read or write those bits.

For a solid state drive, NAND[2] flash memory has transistors arranged in a grid, where a cell (the intersection of a row and column) is in either a high-voltage or a low-voltage state.

Each disk has a controller, a component that manages the physical details of accessing the media and enables the CPU to simply request the desired data rather than know how to physically manipulate the actuator arm of the hard drive or apply voltages to the transistors of the solid state drive. The controller may perform additional functions such as detecting and remapping bad sectors, detecting and correcting errors, and wear leveling.[3]

Down in the weeds

All flash memory uses transistors to store data, but those transistors may be arranged in different ways. The two main types, NOR and NAND,

---

[1]Traditionally 512 bytes for hard disks, but 4096 bytes has been standard since 2011, with eight 512-byte sections combined into one data field.

[2]Not AND - see Down in the weeds box.

[3]In wear leveling, the controller attempts to arrange data so that writes are distributed evenly across the drive, as flash memory can only be written a limited number of times before becoming unreliable.

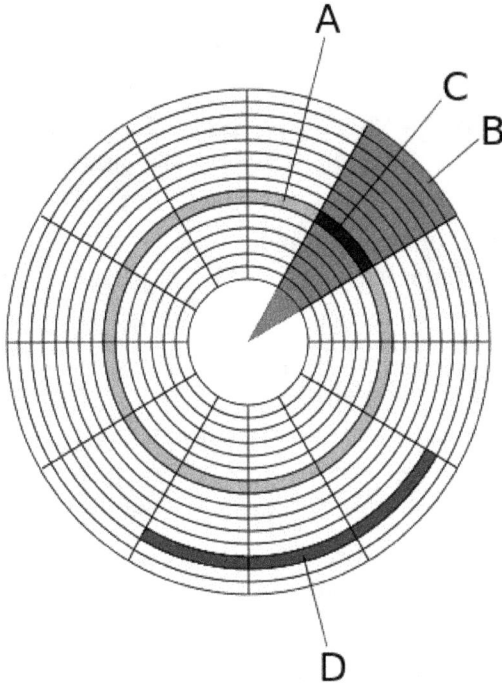

Figure 24.1: An illustration of a hard drive platter. Each concentric circle [A] is called a track; each pie slice [B] is a geometrical sector. The intersection of a track and a geometrical sector is a track sector [C] and is the smallest section that can be read or written. A block [D] is the smallest logical amount of disk space that will actually be used by the operating system (for example, to store a file). Public domain image from wikimedia commons.

are named after the logic gates they mimic. The different arrangements of transistors lead to different physical properties, as described below.

NOR (Not OR) flash memory provides random access, high-speed reads, high reliability, and the ability to read or write single bytes.

NAND (Not AND) flash has smaller cells, which results in much higher write and erase speeds, as well as lower costs. However, NAND flash is accessed in pages or blocks rather than bytes. As NAND flash uses an indirect interface, it is more complicated to access, and the presence of bad blocks requires additional error-correcting functionality that isn't necessary for NOR flash.

In practice, NOR flash is used for code storage and execution, such as the firmware on cell phones, while NAND flash is used for data storage, such as memory sticks and solid state drives.

24.2   Data and I/O

The physical structures of hard disks and NAND drives do not allow us to read or write a single byte; rather, we deal with an entire block at once. A *block* is the smallest unit of data that the operating system can logically read or write, while a *sector* is the smallest unit of data that can be physically read from or written to the disk; thus, the size of a block is equal to the size of one or more sectors. Depending on the disk, this is generally 512 or

4096 bytes.[4]

An SSD has no sectors, but the memory cells are divided into pages, where several (generally 128) pages make up a block. Data can be read and written at the page level but can only be erased at the block level.

Each physical sector has a header, which contains information used by the drive controller, and a data area, which contains both the actual user data and error-correcting code (ECC). The header takes up a relatively smaller percentage of larger sectors, making the sectors more efficient (a larger percentage of the drive can be allocated to user data). Larger sectors do require more ECC bytes to maintain the same error-correcting rate. Additionally, as information is stored more densely on higher-capacity hard drives, any physical flaw will affect a correspondingly larger number of bits, again requiring more ECC bits to maintain the same error correction rate.

24.3   Memory

The primary detail of interest to programmers discussing computer memory (aside from why there isn't more of it) will be how it is allocated. Information in an executing program is stored on either the (control) stack or the heap. In either case, the item is stored in memory (with a caveat noted below); the stack and heap are simply the data structures we use to keep track of it.

When a program is running and calls a function, all of

---

[4]Disks using 4096-byte sectors can generally emulate 512-byte sectors. However, this still involves reading and writing the entire 4096-byte sector to update the logical 512 bytes, with a corresponding decrease in speed.

that function's variables go on the stack. When the function exits, all of its variables are removed from the stack and that memory can be reused. The stack also holds pointers to function calls to allow execution to return to the correct location.

Because a stack is a simple last-in, first-out data structure (as discussed in Section 2.4), allocating and reclaiming memory is more efficient than when using a heap.[5] In a multi-threaded application, each thread gets its own stack. As the stack tends to hold a (relatively) small number of items and the memory in the stack is accessed frequently, values in the stack are likely to be cached. Additionally, research shows that a small stack cache (separate from the main cache) leads to significant performance improvements.[6]

Only primitives and references are placed on the stack; objects are always placed in the heap.[7] Whereas memory access for the stack is strictly regulated, any element in the heap can be accessed at any time; there is no ordering of the various objects. The heap and the stack are both stored in memory; often the stack grows downward from the highest-available memory address, while the heap grows upward from the lowest-available address.

Unlike the stack, memory on the heap is dynami-

---

[5]When a function returns, all of the memory it was allocated on the stack is automatically reclaimed.

[6]M. Schoeberl and C. Nielsen, "A Stack Cache for Real-Time Systems," 2016 IEEE 19th International Symposium on Real-Time Distributed Computing (ISORC), York, 2016, pp. 150-157.

[7]This is not the same as the heap data structure; it's just an area of memory that's allocated differently from the stack. When the *new* (in C++) or *malloc* (in C) command is used to allocate memory, that memory comes from the heap.

cally allocated and can be released at any time.[8] The heap is less efficient to access, and memory must be tracked rather than being automatically reclaimed, but it can hold objects of variable size, and objects can persist across stack levels.

24.4 Cache

While RAM is much faster than disk, it's still not able to provide data to the CPU immediately. One reason for this is the speed-of-light limit: light (and thus, data) can only travel so far in a given amount of time.[9] In a vacuum, light travels at approximately one foot per nanosecond.[10] This means that if a CPU is operating at 3GHz, the absolute furthest a signal could travel in one clock cycle is four inches, round trip. As a result, if the memory is located more than two inches away from the CPU, data can not be retrieved within one clock cycle, even if the memory responds instantly.

Of course, memory does not actually respond instantly. Another factor is how long it takes for a memory module to access a particular location.[11] Even with very fast RAM, the latency means there will be a multiple-nanosecond delay between when information is requested

---

[8]When you create an object, memory is allocated for it on the heap. When you release the memory (or the object is garbage collected), that memory is again available for use.

[9]The speed of light is of course a hard limit; that doesn't mean we're actually transferring data that quickly, only that this is the maximum speed at which the data could possibly travel.

[10]See Admiral Grace Hopper explain the nanosecond at https://www.youtube.com/watch?v=9eyFDBPk4Yw.

[11]This is CAS (column address strobe) latency.

and when it is available.

We handle both of these problems by locating a small amount of very fast memory on the die itself.[12] As this memory is very close to the processor, we minimize the speed-of-light delay, and because we use a small amount of very fast memory, we minimize the lag as well. Only so much memory will fit on the die, and the fast memory used is expensive,[13] so we use it to cache frequently-used data. This on-die memory is the L1 cache; there may also be an L2 cache that is still on the motherboard but may not be on the chip itself.[14]

24.5   Registers

While computers attempt to use cache memory to hold data for the near future, registers are used to hold data and instructions for right now. Registers are the memory that the processor actually works with directly, and are naturally made up of the memory that is closest to the CPU and has the fastest response time. In Section 25.1.

---

[12]The die is a piece of semiconductor material on which the transistors making up the CPU reside; together with the embedded electronics, it forms an integrated circuit (generally called a chip). A silicon wafer is produced that contains many CPUs, and then it is diced up to get the individual devices for sale. Each die may contain multiple cores.

[13]Cache memory uses SRAM, which is much faster than the DRAM used for main memory, but takes up more space and is more expensive.

[14]In addition to the increased distance from the processor, L2 cache generally uses slower DRAM memory, but tends to be several times as large (in number of megabytes, if not physical size) as L1 cache.

we'll see an example of a machine code instruction that specifies the register where a value should be placed.

A CPU will generally have both general-purpose registers (which store temporary data and can be accessed by user programs) and specific-use registers, such as the accumulator, program counter, and instruction register.[15]

---

[15]The accumulator stores intermediate results when doing arithmetic; think of it as a scratchpad for when when the result of one calculation is used as input for the next. The program counter contains the address of the next instruction to be fetched from memory. The instruction register contains the instruction currently executing.

Chapter 25

Software Abstractions

25.1 Machine code and assembly language

In the beginning, there was machine code. Machine code is the actual code that runs on the processor and is specific to that family of processors. A binary (or, for the ease of the programmer, hexadecimal) number represents an action to perform and the data to perform it on. Assembly language makes programming easier by replacing the numbers with mnemonics. For example,[1] rather than writing 10110000 01100001 (in binary) or B0 61 (in hexadecimal), we can write MOV AL, 61h. In this case, B0 is a machine language instruction (for an x86/IA-32 processor) that tells the system to move the following value into register AL. MOV AL means the same, but is easier

---

[1]Example taken from the wikipedia page at https://en.wikipedia.org/wiki/Machine_code, because I haven't written assembly in two decades and don't want to start again.

for most of us to read. An assembler converts the assembly language into machine code, which the processor executes.

25.2   Low-level languages

Machine code and assembly language are considered low-level languages, because there is little to no abstraction between the language and what actually gets executed; no compiler or interpreter is required. As a result, code written in a low-level language can be very efficient but will generally be non-portable, as it is designed for a particular family of processors.

25.3   High-level languages

By contrast with low-level languages, high-level languages provide a layer of abstraction, allowing the code to be compiled or interpreted to run on many different machines. This abstraction means that the programmer cannot optimize the code based on the properties of the specific hardware upon which the code will be run. Where performance is extremely important and the target hardware is known, the programmer may choose to write particularly critical code in assembly, but write the rest of the software in a high-level language. In other cases, a programmer with a good understanding of both assembly language and the compiler for a high-level language may simply write high-level code in such a way that the compiler will generate highly efficient compiled code.

When to use assembly language

Programmers who code in assembly language say that it has three advantages. The first two are obvious: the code takes up less space and runs faster. The third is less obvious: when there's a bug, it tends to lead to catastrophic failure. Normally this might not be considered an advantage, but it makes it very obvious that you've screwed up.

The vast majority of the time, it makes more sense to simply work in a high-level language. Assembly can make sense primarily when working with embedded systems with very limited processing power, particularly when the saved space allows for using cheaper processors. In this case, the savings on each processor, for a high-volume application, can more than make up for the additional developer time.

For example, DSP (digital signal processing) programs are often written in assembly.

Chapter 26

Computer Arithmetic

Consider an application that requires making millions of calculations very quickly.

There are several ways we can approach this. One is to build specialized hardware that is optimized for the required operations.[1] Another is to structure the calculations in such a way that they take advantage of operations the computer can do quickly.[2]

---

[1]For example, graphical processing units (GPUs) can do certain types of calculations many times faster than general purpose CPUs. For this reason, they are useful for non-graphical applications as well; for example, bitcoin mining.

[2]Consider the problem of computing reciprocal square roots, which are used in applications such as vector normalization. There is a method to quickly approximate the answer using bit shifting that was used in video games such as Quake. At the time, it was much faster than doing the actual calculations. For details, search 0x5f3759df.

26.1 Bit shifting

The bit shift operators ($<<$ and $>>$ in the C-family languages) shift all bits in a register by one position.

When we shift left, we fill in zeros on the right end of the operand. This has the effect, when left-shifting n bits, of multiplying the number by 2^n.

Right-shifting can be either arithmetic or logical.[3] In an arithmetic right-shift, the left-most bit is duplicated. Given a two's complement[4] signed binary number, right-shifting by n bits is equivalent to dividing by 2^n, rounded down (that is, towards negative infinity). In a logical right-shift, zeros shift in on the right (which is appropriate for unsigned binary numbers).

> **Example - C#**
>
> C# defines the bitwise operators for the int, uint, long, and ulong types. Other types are converted to int (and the bitwise operation returns an int).
>
> For any variable *num* of an appropriate type, *num* $<<$ *x* would left-shift *num* by *x* bits. For example, if *num*=3 (0000 0011), then *num* $<<$ 4 would be 3×2^4=48 (0011 0000).

---

[3]So can left-shifting, but arithmetic and logical left-shifting are equivalent.

[4]The one's complement of a binary number is obtained by toggling all of the bits; the two's complement is obtained from the one's complement by adding one. Generally, a signed number uses two's complement representation: a positive value will have a sign bit of zero and be stored normally, while a negative value will have a sign bit of one and be stored in two's complement form.

> The right-shift operator does an arithmetic shift if the operand is signed and a logical shift if it is not.

Why use bit shifting, when it's logically equivalent to multiplying or dividing by two? Mostly because it's fast. In older code (when space or bandwidth was more of a concern) data would have been packed as tightly as possible and bit-shifted into position for reading (taking a byte one nibble at a time).

26.2   Binary AND and OR

Where logical AND and OR (&& and || in C) take two booleans (or values that can be treated as booleans) and return a truthiness value, binary AND and OR (& and |) take and return bits. ANDing two bits together gives a 1 if both are 1 and a 0 otherwise; ORing them together gives 0 if both are 0 and 1 otherwise.

Example - Masking

Binary operators are often used for masking. Suppose an object has a number of boolean properties. We can combine them into one variable by assigning each to be a power of two and ORing them together:

PropertyOne $= 2^0 = 1 << 0 = 1$
PropertyTwo $= 2^1 = 1 << 1 = 2$
PropertyThree $= 2^2 = 1 << 2 = 4$
PropertyFour $= 2^3 = 1 << 3 = 8$

If an object has properties one, two, and four,

the flag variable will be 0001 | 0010 | 1000 = 1011.

Later on, we want to know whether the object has properties three and four.

Property three: (0100 & 1011) = 0

Property four: (1000 & 1011) = 1

In code, we would have defined the properties as constants, and would just write the following[a]

if ((PropertyThree & flagVar) !=0)

if ((PropertyFour & flagVar) != 0)

If we want to check multiple properties at once, we can OR all of them together into a new sumVar and AND it with flagVar. If the result is sumVar, every boolean returned true.

---

[a]Yes, the !=0 is unnecessary in C, as zero is interpreted as false and anything else is interpreted as true, but treating a number as if it were a boolean can lead to odd bugs.

26.3   Binary NOT

The binary NOT operation ($\sim$) flips the bits in a number; 1s become 0s and 0s become 1s.

Example - More masking

Continuing the example above, we now want PropertyFour to be set to false. We take the NOT of PropertyFour to get $\sim$1000=0111 and AND it with flagVAR. 0111 & 1011 = 0011. We now have only the first two properties set, as desired.

26.4   Exclusive OR

The logical exclusive OR (XOR or ˆ) returns true if exactly one of its operands is true; the binary version returns 1 if exactly one operand is 1.

A consequence of this is that XOR is reversible; applying the operation twice will return the original value. For example, consider a plaintext 10100101 that we wish to encrypt using a one-time pad[5] 10110111.

- To encrypt the message, we XOR it with the pad: 10100101 XOR 10110111 gives us a ciphertext of 00010010.

- To decrypt the ciphertext, XORing it with the pad gives us 00010010 XOR 10110111 = 10100101, which was the original message.

Outside of cryptography, this is useful for solving problems with a minimal amount of storage space. One popular example is to find the only non-repeated element in a list of repeated elements: we XOR together every value in the list and the repeated ones cancel each other out (any value XORed by itself is zero) to leave the unique value.[6] Another is swapping the contents of two variables without using a temporary variable: let $x = x$ XOR y, $y = y$ XOR x, and then $x = x$ XOR y.[7]

---

[5]We cover one–time pads in Section 21.3.

[6]Obviously this trick requires that every repeated value is repeated an even number of times.

[7]The first XOR gives us everything that is in exactly one of x or y. The second gives us everything that is in exactly one or exactly three of x or y or y; that is, x. The third XOR then gives us everything that is in exactly one or three of x or y or x - that is, y. You should generally just use a temporary variable.

Chapter 27

Operating Systems

The operating system can be thought of as another layer of abstraction, separating the user (or programmer) from the physical structure of the computer. Rather than managing the hardware directly, application code can simply call into operating system APIs to invoke system functionality.

27.1 Process management

As a general rule, users like to do more than one thing at a time.[1] Like the human brain, a computer processor can only work on one task at a time,[2] but switches between tasks to give the appearance of doing many things simultaneously. This switching allows the tasks to share system resources (including CPUs and memory), but re-

---

[1]Citation needed.

[2]Modern CPUs tend to have multiple cores, where each core is a full processor that can handle tasks independently.

quires additional work to switch contexts[3] and ensure
that no *process* (the execution of a task) interferes with
any other.

27.1.1 Multitasking

A multitasking system works by time-sharing, where the
processing capability is divided into time slices and those
slices are assigned to the various processes. Modern computers generally use preemptive multitasking, where the
kernel will interrupt the currently-executing process when
its time slice is up or when a higher priority task needs
the processor. As the operating system controls the allocation of time slices, each process can be guaranteed to
eventually receive CPU time. However, any given process may lose control at any time, and it is possible for
several processes using shared resources to deadlock, in
which case no deadlocked process can finish its execution
because each one is waiting on a resource held by another
process in the group.

> **Example**
> The usual example is the dining philosophers
> problem, in which five silent
> (non-communicating) philosophers sit around a
> table eating spaghetti, with one fork between each
> pair of philosophers. Each philosopher either eats
> or thinks; if he eats, he takes the forks from both

---

[3]The context of a process is its current state, including the
contents of all registers that will be needed when execution resumes.
This information is saved to the Process Control Block (PCB),
which will be used to restore the state when the process restarts.

sides. A philosopher with only one fork will not eat, but will wait for the second fork to become available; thus, if each philosopher picks up the fork on his left, all will starve while waiting for the second fork to be released.

In another style, cooperative multitasking, each process controls its own time and voluntarily yields control either periodically or when logically blocked (such as when waiting for I/O). Cooperative multitasking relies on all processes regularly surrendering control and is impractical on most systems, as a process that declines to yield can starve other processes. However, it is commonly used in embedded systems.[4]

27.1.2 Multiprocessing and multithreading

When one computer contains multiple processors, several of those processes can actually run simultaneously (rather than in time slices), one per processor. Alternatively, one process can have multiple threads running on different processors. Multithreading can increase program responsiveness, lead to better utilization of system resources, and allow for parallelization. However, multithreaded applications can be more difficult to program due to the need to carefully synchronize the threads to avoid race conditions.[5]

---

[4]We discuss embedded systems in Chapter 29.

[5]The author can say from experience that race conditions in multithreaded programs can be an enormous pain to debug.

27.1.3   Multithreading and race conditions

Race conditions occur when two or more threads try to change shared data at the same time. The result of the change depends on the order in which the threads happen to access the shared data. Often something like this happens:

1. Thread A encounters an *if* statement and checks the conditional.

2. Thread B executes code that would change the result of the conditional.

3. Thread A continues executing the body of the *if* statement, even though it is no longer appropriate.

To avoid Heisenbug,[6] we need to do one of the following:

- Lock the shared data prior to accessing it with either thread and thus ensure that it does not change while in use.[7]

- Make the entire unit of work (both the conditional and the body of the *if* statement) an atomic operation, meaning that it cannot be interrupted.[8]

---

[6]The bug that occurs only when you're not looking for it.

[7]C# has the *Interlocked* class, which provides atomic operations.

[8]In Java, we use the *synchronized* keyword to ensure that only one thread can execute a block of code at a time.

27.2 Storage management

We previously discussed[9] how memory is allocated on either the stack or the heap. The operating system must manage this memory, determining which memory to assign to which process and when to reclaim it.

27.2.1 Logical and Physical Addresses

Suppose that a new process is created and will be allowed to use 4 GB of memory. If we give the process direct memory access, we run into several problems.

- How do we ensure that the process does not access any memory outside of the allowed block?

- If we do not have a contiguous 4 GB block of RAM, how do we create one?

- If the process is suspended and its RAM is used by another process, do we need to wait until that specific block of memory is available again before the process can resume?

The solution is replacing physical memory with logical memory. Rather than giving each process direct access to a range of physical memory addresses, we assign it a block of logical memory addresses, which the CPU can then map to physical addresses. As a result, the process does not need to know anything about where its data is actually stored.[10] The data for the process can be

---

[9]Section 24.3.

[10]For more details on dynamic memory allocation, see Section 2.5 of *The Art of Computer Programming* by Donald Knuth.

moved around as desired without the risk that the process will (deliberately or accidentally) access memory outside of its assigned space. Infrequently used items can be moved to swap space, while still appearing to the process to be in RAM. If multiple processes need a copy of the same instructions, the same physical memory can map to multiple logical addresses.

27.2.2   Paging and Swapping

> Data expands to fill the space available for storage.
>
> - Parkinson's Law of Data

Assuming that the system's RAM is not large enough to simultaneously keep the data for all running processes in memory, what is the solution? One option is swapping: load a process entirely into memory, run it until control passes to a different process, and then write it back to disk so that the memory is available for the next process to run. Alternatively, we can load only those parts of each program that are currently required into memory, leaving the rest on disk until we need them.

With paging, the virtual address space is broken down into fixed-size units called pages, which map onto page frames (of the same size) in memory. Whenever a program attempts to make a memory access, we index into the page table to find the location of the appropriate page frame in memory. If that page is not currently loaded, a page fault occurs; we then load the appropriate frame (replacing another page currently in memory as needed).

Practical considerations of paging

When a page needs to be loaded and there is no space available, how do we make room? Ideally we would like to replace a page that we won't need again. Since it's generally impractical to determine which pages we'll need in the future, we can instead replace pages we haven't used recently.

Each page has flags set that show whether a process has read or modified it, with the read bit being cleared periodically. When we need space, we randomly remove a page that has not been recently accessed, under the assumption it is less likely to be needed again in the near future.[a] If the page has been modified, we write those changes back to disk.

---

[a]We actually divide pages into four categories: not referenced or modified, modified but not referenced, referenced but not modified, and referenced and modified. A page can be modified but not referenced because the read bit is cleared periodically, but the modified bit (which is needed to determine whether we must write the page back to disk) is not. When we need to remove a page, we choose one from the lowest nonempty class, so a page that has been modified but not recently accessed will be removed before one that has been accessed recently but not modified.

Often a process will be working with a small set of its available pages.[11] If this entire *working set* is in memory, the process can execute quickly despite having only a

---

[11]Locality of reference, previously mentioned in Section 2.2.

small number of pages loaded. However, if only part of the working set is loaded at a time, the result will be frequent page faults as the process continuously finds that the page it needs is not in memory (*thrashing*). To avoid this, we may allow a process to run only when its entire working set can be loaded into memory.[12] If there is insufficient memory available to hold the current working sets of all running processes, then some processes should be swapped out to avoid thrashing.

27.3   I/O

An important function of the operating system is providing a uniform view of I/O devices. From the standpoint of a process, it should not matter whether data is read from memory, from disk, or from the network, or whether it is written to the screen, to a file, or to a printer. The operating system provides an interface that allows the process to simply read from standard input or write to standard output.

From an operating system perspective, I/O tends to be extremely slow compared to processor speed.[13] For a simple system that does only one thing at a time, it may be sufficient for the processor to request I/O and then *busy wait*[14] until the appropriate device has processed

---

[12]To avoid page faults we may load the entire working set before allowing the process to resume; this is called prepaging.

[13]There are exceptions, such as Oracle's Exadata servers, but most of us are not prepared to spend hundreds of thousands of dollars (or more) for a server.

[14]When a process busy waits, it simply checks a condition repeatedly, using up CPU cycles without accomplishing anything until the condition is met; this is also called *spinning*.

the data. In most cases, we prefer that the processor do a context switch and come back to the current process when I/O is complete. One way to switch back is to have the hardware interrupt the CPU whenever it is ready for the next character, but this wastes a significant amount of time, as interrupts are expensive. A better option is the use of a direct memory access (DMA) controller. The CPU simply initiates the transfer, hands it off to the DMA controller, then is interrupted only when the transfer is complete.

27.4   Security

In Chapter 20, we discussed the three elements of computer security: confidentiality, integrity, and availability. In terms of operating systems, we can consider it the system's job to ensure that data belonging to a user or process is not accessed by another user or process without permission, that it is not altered unexpectedly, and that it is available on request.

In the sections above, we discussed ensuring that a process is able to access only the memory locations allocated to it by the operating system and is not able to monopolize the CPU. As a general rule, we wish to ensure that each process accesses only those resources it is permitted to use, in ways that it is permitted to use them.

This is done by requiring that processes access resources by sending a request to the operating system, rather than taking control of the hardware directly. The operating system must then verify that the request is appropriate. This verification can be done with access control lists (ACLs), which identify the processes that can use a resource and in what ways, or with capability lists, which determine the access granted to a given process.

In order to ensure that processes cannot bypass the access control measures, it is crucial to avoid the operating system itself being corrupted. In trusted computing systems, we create a trusted computing base (TCB) consisting of those components (both hardware and software) that are responsible for maintaining security. The TCB is kept as small as possible to make it possible to verify correctness; all requests for system resources must go through the reference monitor, which acts as a barrier between the trusted and untrusted parts of the system.

More generally, computer security works based on the principle of least privilege: every actor (be that a process, user, or program) should have the amount of access required for its purpose and no more. Thus, the kernel[15] is kept as small as possible and is isolated from everything else on the system.

Programs execute as user-level processes, which do not have permission to access resources directly. When access is needed, the process makes a system call, interrupting the kernel. After verifying that the process has access to the requested resource, the kernel performs the desired access.

---

[15]The kernel is the part of the operating system that is always in memory and has full access to all system resources.

Chapter 28

Distributed Systems

Consider building a popular search engine. As it grows we encounter several challenges:

- Scalability - the system must handle an ever-increasing amount of data.

- Performance - the system should not slow down as demands on it increase.

- Availability - the system must always be available; downtime is unacceptable.

We can improve performance and scalability to a point by throwing more hardware at the problem, but eventually we reach the limits of what a single system can handle.[1] The solution is to divide the work among multiple less expensive computers. This provides scalability

---

[1] We reach the limits of what a reasonably-priced computer can handle rather sooner.

(as demand increases, we can add more servers), performance (each server must handle only a limited amount of demand), and availability (redundant servers allow us to immediately switch to a replacement when one fails). Even a smaller system may benefit from breaking up components onto multiple machines: a web server, a database server, and so forth.

Scaling Google

When Google started in 1998, they had four computers and several hundred gigabytes of storage space. They now run more than two million servers in multiple data centers around the world.

28.1 The fallacies of distributed computing

Distributed computing brings its own challenges. L. Peter Deutsch and others[2] have created a list of false assumptions that new distributed systems programmers often make:[3]

1. **Assumption**: The network is reliable.
   Reality: The network (or critical parts) will go offline at inconvenient times.

2. **Assumption**: Latency is zero.
   Reality: Packets will be delayed.

---

[2]See https://web.archive.org/web/20070811082651/http://java.syscon.com/read/38665.htm for a brief history.

[3]See https://www.rgoarchitects.com/Files/fallacies.pdf for more details and examples.

Historical aside - Latency

There is a famous story about a department at the University of North Carolina in the 90s that one day found they couldn't send email more than about 500 miles. The sysadmin obviously thinks this can't possibly be true, but he starts testing and verifies it. Eventually he figures out that the email server was upgraded, no longer understood the config file, and was timing out almost immediately - in just enough time for a message to reach, and be acknowledged by, a system up to 500 miles away.

3. **Assumption**: Bandwidth is infinite.
   Reality: Data will experience congestion.

4. **Assumption**: The network is secure.
   Reality: Hackers will try to steal your data.

Historical aside - Security

In 2013, one of the documents released by Edward Snowden revealed that the NSA was intercepting data being sent between data centers owned by Google (and Yahoo). Google responded by encrypting the data links connecting its data centers.

In 2014, several security engineers independently discovered a bug (called Heartbleed) in OpenSSL would allow an attacker to steal

> information normally protected by the SS-L/TLS encryption. As of November 2019, the Shodan Heartbleed Report found that 91,063 public web servers were still vulnerable to Heartbleed.

5. **Assumption**: Topology doesn't change.
   Reality: Nodes will be added and/or removed from the network.

6. **Assumption**: There is one administrator.
   Reality: Different administrators will set different policies.

7. **Assumption**: Transport cost is zero.
   Reality: Moving data between nodes will have a cost.

> **Historical aside - Transport cost**
>
> In 2013, Comcast and Verizon internet customers started seeing lower quality streaming video, to the point where many dropped Netflix. In early 2014, Netflix reached agreements with both carriers to pay for direct connections to their networks.

8. **Assumption**: The network is homogeneous.
   Reality: Different parts of the system will use different hardware.

To these I will also add:

9. **Assumption**: We can tell in what order events have occurred.
   Reality: Different servers may disagree on what happened first.

We discuss these challenges in the sections that follow.

28.2 Communication

The various processes that make up a distributed system will communicate with each other by passing messages. Any two processes could be located on the same machine or on two servers thousands of miles apart. The system designers must make decisions that include:

- Should we require that messages be acknowledged, and if so, how long should we wait for the acknowledgement?

- Do we want to receive each message at least once, or at most once?

- How do we respond if some elements of the system become unavailable?

- How do we handle the addition or removal of servers?

Simply put, a distributed system must take into account what will happen when messages cannot be delivered in a timely, reliable, or secure manner, or can't be delivered at all.

28.3 Synchronization and consistency

Consider what happens when data is replicated across multiple geographically dispersed servers. This replication reduces latency (the closest server will, on average, be closer than if only one central server was used) and provides redundancy (if one server goes down, the others are still available). It also raises the question of how to keep the servers in sync when data changes.

If only one server may accept edits (with all the others being read-only), that one server still represents a single point of failure. If every server allows both reads and writes, it is possible for multiple servers to be updated at approximately the same time and contain conflicting information. Even if data is edited on only one server, the other servers will receive updates from it at different times, so a user may see different values depending on which server he queries.

If multiple servers receive conflicting updates, there must be a policy for which one to accept. Due to the lack of a universal clock, it may not be possible to determine which update actually occurred first, and the various servers may receive them in different orders.

Why is there no universal clock?
Many things in distributed systems would be much simpler if we knew exactly when events occurred. However, each system will have its own clock, and the clocks may run at slightly different rates. We can synchronize all of the clocks

with one trusted clock, but because the time it takes to receive a message from the trusted clock varies, our assorted systems still will not be perfectly in sync.

Chapter 29

Embedded Systems

To the average (non-programmer) person, "computer" means a general-purpose computer, something that can run a wide variety of programs. However, general-purpose computers make up only a small fraction[1] of all computers. Most are embedded systems, which are systems that are purpose-built for a particular application. These tiny computers operate everything from your microwave to even the rearview mirror and headlights of some cars.[2] Embedded systems programming is what you do when you want your software to control hardware directly.

Programming for embedded systems means being more resource-constrained than with most general applications. An embedded system often has a limited amount of power and memory, a slow processor, and a limited number of peripherals. It may need to operate indefinitely without being serviced (consider a system embedded in a satel-

---

[1]By some estimates, the percentage approaches zero.

[2]See https://patents.google.com/patent/US8625815B2/en and https://www.cs.cmu.edu/smartheadlight/ for a few examples.

lite or dropped into the Mariana Trench). It might need to recover gracefully from errors or it might be required to fail catastrophically the first time an error occurs. It may need to react deterministically (always responding in the exact same way to a given input) or within a maximum amount of time.[3] Designing an embedded system generally involves making trade-offs between various constraints.

One challenge in embedded systems programming is that development generally cannot be done on the same hardware that will run the software. An embedded system generally doesn't have extra capacity for running a debugger and likely can't drive a monitor or typical input devices directly; instead, we program them using a general-purpose computer.

The limited resources available increase the usefulness of methods such as those described in Chapter 26, which increase program speed at the possible expense of clarity.

---

[3]Many embedded systems use real-time operating systems, which are required to process data within fixed time constraints; the primary design goal is a performance guarantee, where speed and predictability are more valued than throughput.

Getting started with embedded systems

The standard for embedded systems development has long been the Arduino,[a] an open-source physical computing platform. While the platform is inexpensive (an entry-level board costs around $20) and appropriate for students and hobbyists,[b] it's also a powerful tool for creating real products.[c]

---

[a]The image is an Arduino Uno R3. Taken by Spark-Fun, released under Creative Commons license.

[b]See https://create.arduino.cc/projecthub for everything from games to robots.

[c]See https://www.arduino.cc/pro/verticals for different areas in which Arduinos have been used professionally.

Chapter 30

Networks and the Internet

Modern software often is written to operate over a computer network (usually the internet). From software as a service (SaaS) to MMORPGS, from networked printers to security cameras with automatic offsite backups, our software and devices depend on being able to quickly, reliably, and securely communicate with other devices that may be across the room or across the world.

There are two widely-used models for describing how networks are built, each of which divides functionality into various layers that can be set up independently of the others. For example, your email client doesn't care how the email reaches its destination. The router that forwards the packets doesn't care what they contain. The ethernet cable is concerned simply with transferring bits from one end to the other. Each layer has its own *protocols*, which are rules that specify how data should be handled at that level.

The TCP/IP model has four layers built around the TCP/IP protocols, on which the internet was developed. The OSI model is a more generic, theoretical model, offering seven protocol layers and guidelines rather than standards.

30.1 Protocol Layers

30.1.1 Application layer

At the top of the stack, the application layer provides process-to-process communication, allowing applications to communicate over whatever network is present. This layer includes protocols such as HTTP, FTP, and SMTP. Lower layers are largely treated as a black box that provides a connection over which the application layer may transfer data.

This layer in the TCP/IP model encompasses three layers in the OSI model:

- Layer 7, the application layer, is what the user interacts with directly (e.g., web browser).

- Layer 6, the presentation layer, formats the data from layer 7 so that it is ready to be handed off to the network (or formats network data for the application). For example, the data may be encrypted or decrypted.

- Layer 5, the session layer, sets up a session between the two communicating devices.

30.1.2 Transport layer

The transport layer provides end-to-end message transfer services that are independent of both the data to be transferred and the logistics of physically moving that data over the network. The transport layer offers either connection-oriented (TCP) or connectionless (UDP) transmission. This layer is responsible for determining quality of service (that is, how we handle packets that are lost or mishandled by the network).

30.1.3 Internet or network layer

The internet layer (in TCP/IP) or network layer (in OSI) is where packets are routed from one device to the next. At this level, the Internet Protocol (IPv4 or IPv6) is used to transfer data.

30.1.4 Link layer

A link includes all hosts (devices) that can be accessed without passing through a router; the link layer moves packets between hosts on the same link. In the OSI model, this is broken down into two layers:

- Layer 2, the data link layer, provides node-to-node data transfer and handles errors from the physical layer.

- Layer 1, the physical layer, is the actual cables, voltages, and radio signals involved in transferring the data.

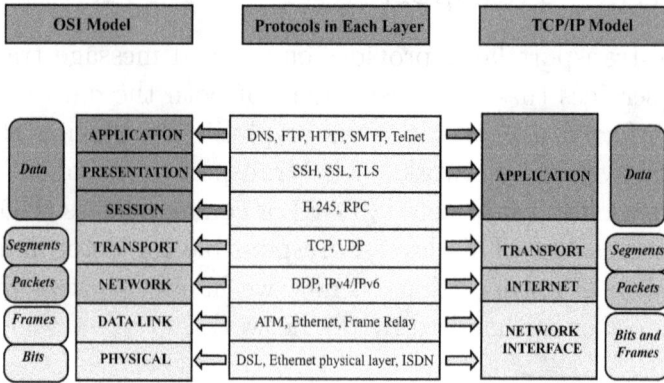

OSI Model		Protocols in Each Layer	TCP/IP Model	
Data	APPLICATION	DNS, FTP, HTTP, SMTP, Telnet	APPLICATION	Data
	PRESENTATION	SSH, SSL, TLS		
	SESSION	H.245, RPC		
Segments	TRANSPORT	TCP, UDP	TRANSPORT	Segments
Packets	NETWORK	DDP, IPv4/IPv6	INTERNET	Packets
Frames	DATA LINK	ATM, Ethernet, Frame Relay	NETWORK INTERFACE	Bits and Frames
Bits	PHYSICAL	DSL, Ethernet physical layer, ISDN		

Figure 30.1: A comparison of the OSI and TCP/IP models.

30.2   TCP/IP and UDP

As mentioned above, the transport layer offers the choice of connection-oriented or connectionless communication. With connection-oriented communication, a session is set up between two devices prior to transferring data. Maintaining the session requires that the devices involved hold state information in order to keep the connection open. With connectionless communication, the sender simply sends out the message whenever it is ready, without making prior arrangements.

Connection-oriented protocols are generally used to provide reliable network services, which guarantee that the data will be delivered (or, at least, let the sender know if the data cannot be delivered). These protocols are used when we want to be sure the data arrives safely and is reassembled in the correct order.

88

Connectionless protocols make no guarantees that data will not be lost, mangled, duplicated, or delivered out of order (although these services could be provided at a higher level). Because of the minimal service they provide, connectionless protocols have low overhead and are used when throughput is more important than reliability.

User Datagram Protocol (UDP) and Internet Protocol (IP) are both connectionless protocols; Transmission Control Protocol (TCP) is connection-oriented. We generally refer to Transmission Control Protocol over Internet Protocol, or TCP/IP.[1]

30.3   Delivering a message

We mentioned above that at the network layer, packets are routed from the source to the destination. The internet protocol defines how packets sent over the internet are (hopefully) delivered to their destination.

Consider data that is to be sent over the internet using TCP/IP. At each layer of the protocol model, the data to be transferred is referred to as a *protocol data unit*, or PDU, but it will be formatted in different ways.

From the application perspective, the sender transmits the data and it is delivered to the receiver. At this step, the PDU is a complete message (file/email/etc.) to be transferred.

The transport layer provides a logical connection between two processes running on different hosts; the actual location of those hosts and the nature of the physical link

---

[1]HTTP/1.1 and HTTP/2 operate over TCP; HTTP/3 uses QUIC, which is based on UDP but provides functionality similar to TCP with reduced latency.

between them is immaterial. Here the message from the application layer is broken up into segments that are sized appropriately for the network layer below. Each segment begins with a segment header that contains a variety of information, most notably the port number to which the segment should be delivered.

While the transport layer provided a logical connection between two processes, the network layer provides a logical connection between two hosts (each of which could have many running processes). At this level, the segment from the transport layer is encased in a packet, which includes various data needed to deliver it to the correct location, including the IP addresses of the sending and receiving hosts. While the segment is handled only at the source and destination, every router along the way will handle the packet.

The job of a router is to process packets coming in on its incoming links and route them to the appropriate outgoing links. Routing algorithms are used to calculate the path from source to destination; depending on the network service model, the various packets that make up the message may or may not be sent over the same route and may or may not arrive in the same order in which they were sent.

Finally, the link layer is responsible for moving data over a single link - that is, between two nodes (where a node may be a router or a host). At this level, the packet is encapsulated in a frame, which is physically transmitted from one node to the next.

30.4 Routing algorithms

At the network layer, routing algorithms are used to determine good paths between senders and receivers. A "good" path is one that has the least cost,[2] subject to policy issues (such as where company A refuses to forward packets coming from company B).

We can think of the network as a weighted graph,[3] where the vertices of the graph are places where the packets can be forwarded towards their destination and the edge weights are the costs to use that link.[4]

We categorize routing algorithms in several ways:

- They can be *centralized*, in which the algorithm has global knowledge of the network and calculates the complete path, or *decentralized*, in which each node knows the costs of the path through its direct neighbors (those which are adjacent in the graph) but not the entire path to be taken.

- They can be *static*, in which the routes rarely change (and are often configured manually), or *dynamic*, where the routing paths change according to network traffic and topology updates.[5]

- They can be *load-sensitive*, where costs are adjusted according to network congestion, or *load-*

---

[2]See Section 6.5 on shortest paths.

[3]We cover weighted graphs in Section 4.8.

[4]Cost here could mean a variety of things, from the time taken to transmit over that link to the monetary cost of using it.

[5]Dynamic routing algorithms will respond to changes more quickly, but can run into problems like loops.

insensitive, where they are not.[6]

---

[6]The original ARPAnet routing algorithms were load-sensitive, but modern routing algorithms such as BGP are not.

Chapter 31

Databases

Consider a typical application for manipulating data, such as an inventory system. It would generally need to be able to create or retrieve records, modify them, and then store them again for later retrieval. This is the classic CRUD app - create, read, update, and delete. A database is a way to organize structured information (data) for storage and retrieval.

31.1   Relational databases

Most databases in use today are relational databases. A relational database is organized as a set of related tables, which can be combined using keys.

For example, a business might have a Customers table that lists relevant information about each customer, including an ID. The ID is the primary key - a field[1] that is required for each record and is also unique to that

---

[1]or set of fields

CUST_NAME	*CUST_ID*	ADDRESS
Captain Hook	1904	Jolly Roger
Billy the Kid	1859	Fort Sumner, NM
Mordred	1136	Camelot

Table 31.1: The Customers table in a relational database. CUST_ID (italicized) is the primary key.

ORDER_ID	CUST_ID	COST	ITEM
1	1904	$27	Hook
2	1904	$4	Eyepatch
3	1136	$0	Sword (stolen)

Table 31.2: The Orders table in a relational database. ORDER_ID (italicized) is the primary key, and CUST_ID is the foreign key.

record.

Customer orders are located in an Orders table, which contains all of the information for the order. Rather than putting customer information in the Orders table (which would result in a lot of duplicate information, especially if one customer places many orders), each row has a customer ID that matches the appropriate ID from the Customers table. This is a foreign key - the same ID might be used for many entries in the Orders table, but must map to exactly one entry in the Customers table.

A correctly designed relational database promotes accuracy by avoiding duplication, as in the Customer example above. We store a piece of information only in the appropriate table and link to it as needed.

Common relational database management systems (RDBMSs) include Microsoft SQL Server, Oracle, and MySQL. Like most other relational database systems, they use SQL (structured query language), which is the standard language for querying relational databases. SQL is a declarative language: rather than defining how to do something, you declare what you want to have happen and the computer determines how to accomplish the task.

> **Example**
> Suppose I need to see all orders placed between March 15 and April 1 of last year. I request that information, and then the computer determines how to actually sort the data on the Orders table to find what I'm looking for.

A given RDBMS will generally support both SQL (which is an ANSI standard) and additional proprietary commands. Microsoft (with T-SQL) and Oracle (with PL/SQL) both allow procedural programming and variables in addition to the usual declarative programming supported in standard SQL.

31.2   Hierarchical databases

A hierarchical database organizes data into trees rather than tables. These are used when the application requires being able to quickly pull together all of the relevant information for a particular record, rather than a subset of the available information from many records. For example, electronic medical records are often stored in a hierarchical database to allow quick access to a patient's medical history. If we need to run analytical reports (where finding data about populations rather than

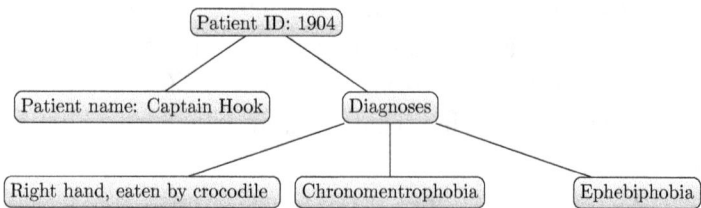

Figure 31.1: A sample patient record in a hierarchical database.

individual patients is required), we may then extract the data to a relational database.

Part XI

Advanced Topics

Chapter 32

The Master Theorem

In Section 1.7, we discussed finding the runtime of simple algorithms. Here we discuss finding the runtime of recursive algorithms.

Consider a divide-and-conquer algorithm, in which a problem is broken down into a number of independent subproblems, which are recursively solved and combined to return a solution to the base problem.

We describe the runtime of the algorithm according to three terms:

- The number of subproblems a that the problem will be broken into.

- The size n/b of each of the smaller subproblems, where b is an integer greater than one. Each subproblem will be at most this size.

- A function $f(n)$ for the time required to break up the problem into subproblems and then combine the answers to those subproblems to obtain the solution.

The master theorem can be used for algorithms where the runtime can be written in the form

$$T(n) = aT(n/b) + f(n),$$

where $T(n)$ is the total runtime and the other parameters are as described above.

We apply one of three cases, depending on the size of $f(n)$.

> **Math alert**
>
> When you see $\log_b a$, it means the logarithm of a to base b.
>
> When $b=2$, this is the binary logarithm, abbreviated lg. For example, $log_2 8=3$.
>
> Other common bases are 10 (the common logarithm, log) and e (the natural logarithm, ln).

1. If $f(n)$ is asymptotically less[1] than $n^{\log_b a}$, then the runtime for the algorithm is $\Theta(n^{\log_b a})$.

2. If $f(n) = \Theta(n^{\log_b a})$, then the total runtime is $\Theta(n^{\log_b a} \cdot \log n)$.

3. If $f(n)$ is asymptotically greater than $n^{\log_b a}$, meaning that the total time to solve all of the subproblems is less than the time required to combine those solutions, then the runtime is $\Theta(f(n))$.

Here we see that the amount of work required for breaking up the problem and then recombining the subproblems, compared to the amount of work required to

---

[1]Mathematically, we write $f(n) = O(n^{\log_b a - \epsilon})$. ϵ (epsilon) represents an arbitrarily small value.

100

actually solve each subproblem, determines the overall runtime of the algorithm.[2]

We can draw the recursion as a tree with depth $\log_b n$, with a^i nodes at depth i. Then there are $a^{\log_b n} = n^{\log_b a}$ leaves. We compare the number of leaves to the amount of work done at each level, and the larger of the two values determines the solution.

In the first case, the amount of work done in each step is bounded from above by $n^{\log_b a}$. At the extreme case, imagine that $f(n)$ is negligible, so the runtime is asymptotically equal to the number of leaves: $n^{\log_b a}$.

In the third case, the amount of work done at each step is bounded from below by $n^{\log_b a}$, which overwhelms the number of leaves, and the total runtime is $\Theta(f(n))$.

In the second case, neither the number of leaves nor the polynomial $f(n)$ dominates the other (they are asymptotically equal) and the runtime is the amount of work done at each level times the number of levels in the tree, or $\Theta(n^{\log_b a} \cdot \log n)$.

Example: Mergesort

Recall from Section 8.3.2 that mergesort works by dividing an array into two smaller arrays, then recursively sorting those arrays.

When we divide up or recombine arrays, we don't do any special processing, so this takes $O(n)$ time. At each step we divide the array in two, so there are $O(\lg n)$ steps. Multiplying, we get a total runtime of $O(n \lg n)$.

---

[2]For a more rigorous treatment and proof of correctness, see Section 4.6 of *Introduction to Algorithms* by Cormen et al.

If we apply the master theorem, then $f(n) = \Theta(n)$. This is case two above (where a and b are both 2), so the runtime of mergesort is $\Theta(n \lg n)$.

Chapter 33

Amortized Runtime

Suppose you have an empty array of size n, and wish to insert values into it. The first n inserts take O(1) time each. On insert $n+1$, the array is full and must be resized, which requires copying all of the values over to a new, larger array, in time O(n).

Any given insert operation takes as much as O(n) time, but this is only the case when the array must be resized; otherwise, inserting takes constant time. What is the average time required for each insert operation?

If we increase the array size by a constant amount each time, then the number of elements that eventually need to be copied over will dominate the constant, and operations will take, on average, O(n) time.[1]

However, if we double the size of the array each time, then the total time to add n items is $n + n$, and each insert takes an average of $2n \ / \ n = $ O(1) time.

---

[1] If c spaces are added each time, then the total cost to add c new items is $n+c$; each insert thus takes an average of $\frac{n+c}{c}$ time, and since n dominates c, this is O(n).

The insight here is that often we don't actually care how long any given operation takes; what's important is the total time required over all operations. When each expensive operation can be paired with many cheap operations, we can amortize the cost of the expensive operation over all of the cheap ones. Thus, even though any given operation may take $O(n)$ time, the amortized cost may be much lower. In the array example above, simply looking at the worst-case runtime for a given step would lead us to conclude that a series of n inserts would be $O(n^2)$, but the amortized analysis shows that (provided we double the number of elements when resizing the array) it will actually be only $O(n)$.

Chapter 34

Splay Trees

In Section 5.1, we introduced binary search trees, which provide $\Theta(\lg n)$ runtime for common operations provided that the height of the tree is kept to $O(\lg n)$. A splay tree[1] is a self-optimizing binary search tree: it rearranges itself so that recently accessed nodes will be moved close to the root, allowing quicker access, while maintaining an average height of $O(\lg n)$. Thus, frequently used items are readily available, while all items can still be accessed in $O(\lg n)$ time in the average case.

34.1   Concepts

Whenever we access a node x of the splay tree, we perform a splay operation (a series of tree rotations) to move it to the root. When the tree has become unbalanced,

---

[1]For more on splay trees, see Section 4.3 of Robert Tarjan's *Data Structure and Network Algorithms*. For an in-depth look at balanced trees in general, see Section 6.2.3 of Donald Knuth's *The Art of Computer Programming*.

finding a node that is lower down in the tree may take $O(n)$ time, but the tree is then rebalanced by the splay step. The end result is that all basic operations are performed in $O(\lg n)$ amortized time.

> **Aside**
>
> A tree rotation changes the structure of a binary tree (updating which nodes are the children of which other nodes) without altering the order of the elements. If a is the left child of b, and we do a tree rotation so that b is the right child of a, we haven't changed that node b is larger than node a; doing an inorder traversal of the tree before and after the rotation will return the same result.

Each operation is one of three possible steps, depending on three factors:

- Whether x is the left or right child of its parent p.

- Whether p is the root.

- Whether p is the left or right child of its parent g (the grandparent of x).

Until x is the root, we use the above factors to choose between three possible tree rotations.

34.2 Zig

When p is the root, we rotate the edge between x and p.

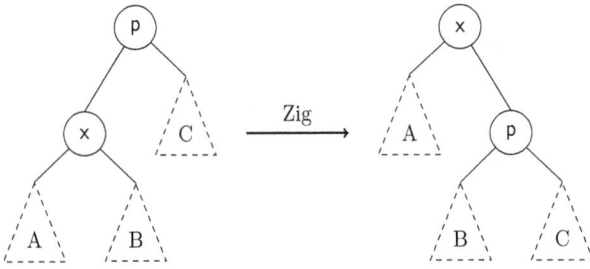

Figure 34.1: After performing the Zig operation, x has become the root.

34.3 Zig-zig

When p is not the root and p and x are both right children or both left children, we rotate the edge between p and g and then rotate the edge between x and p.

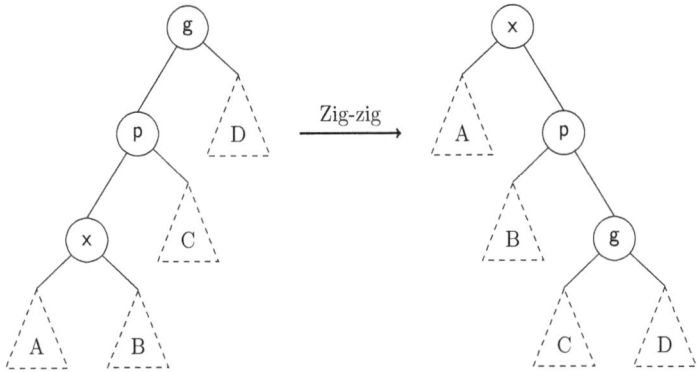

Figure 34.2: After performing the Zig-zig operation, x has replaced its grandparent.

34.4   Zig-zag

When neither of the above cases apply, we rotate on the edge between p and x and then on the resulting edge between x and g.

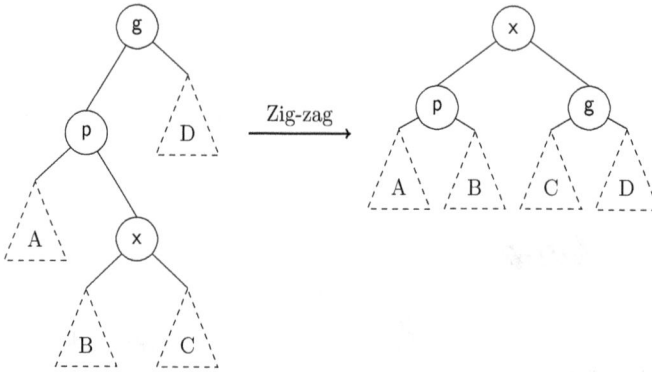

Figure 34.3: After performing the Zig-zag operation, x has again replaced its grandparent.

Chapter 35

Treaps

A treap[1] is another form of self-balancing binary search tree that is a combination of a tree and a heap. Each node has a key value on which the usual binary tree ordering applies. Additionally, each node has a priority on which the heap property applies.

The priority can be assigned either randomly, in which case the treap will have the shape of a random binary tree (and will, with high probability, have height O(log n)), or according to frequency of access, in which case frequently-used nodes would tend to be close to the root.

Searching a treap is identical to searching any other binary search tree, and the priorities are ignored. Adding a new node may require doing tree rotations to maintain the heap property. Deleting a node requires first making it a leaf, if it is not one already; this is done by giving it a priority of negative infinity (-∞) and then doing the appropriate rotations. Once it is a leaf, it can be removed.

---

[1]Raimund Seidel and C.R. Aragon. "Randomized search trees", *Algorithmica*, 16. 1996.

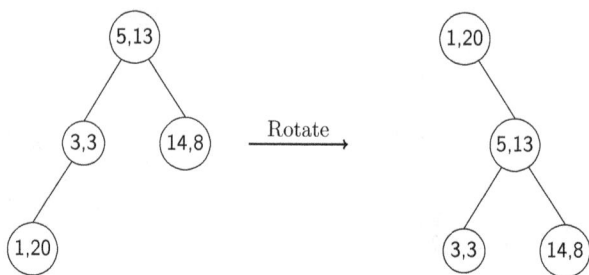

Figure 35.1: After a new node with key 1 and priority 20 is inserted, it is rotated to its proper location in the treap.

In addition to the usual find/insert/delete operations, treaps support union, intersection, and set difference.[2] To accomplish these we define two helper operations.

- Split: This operation splits the treap into two smaller treaps, one with keys less than x and one with keys greater than x. To do this, insert a node with key x and maximum priority. After it is rotated to the top, simply delete it; its former children will be the two desired treaps.

- Join: To join two ordered treaps (treaps where every key in one treap is less than every key in the second treap), create a new node to be the parent of the roots of those treaps. Assign it a legal key (one which is larger than the key of its left child and

---

[2]See Section 2.6 for a review of these terms. For details on performing the set operations and time bounds, see Guy E. Blelloch and Margaret Reid-Miller, "Fast Set Operations Using Treaps", In Proc. 10th Annual ACM SPAA, 1998.

smaller than the key of its right child) and minimum priority. Then rotate it to its proper location (as a leaf) and delete it, leaving behind the desired treap.[3]

Treaps have similar performance to splay trees.

---

[3]Obviously, joins undo splits.

Chapter 36

Artificial Intelligence

Merriam-Webster defines intelligence as the ability to learn, understand, think abstractly, and apply knowledge to manipulate one's environment. Artificial intelligence is the attempt to give a machine those same attributes (or at least, a simulation of them).

We attack the problem in two ways. One is to make computers simulate human (or animal) intelligence so that they will solve problems in the same manner we would. Another is simply to find ways for computers to perform tasks (which we define as requiring intelligence) at least as well as a human could, regardless of how they actually reason about that task. The first approach focuses more on understanding how intelligence works, the second on accomplishing tasks requiring it.

36.1 Types of artificial intelligence

Given an artificial intelligence (AI), how does it solve problems?

A *symbolic* AI has a collection of symbols and rules for manipulating those symbols, which together represent human knowledge in declarative form. The AI uses the rules to manipulate symbols until it reaches the desired outcome. This approach was used to create the General Problem Solver (GPS) in 1959.[1] In theory, the GPS could solve any problem that could be sufficiently specified. In this case, the problem is represented by a directed graph and the computer must determine how to reach one of the vertices which represent a possible answer. A theoretical chess-playing program, for example, wishes to reach one of the end states in which the opponent's king is in checkmate; the rules of the system determine how to move between states.

The GPS was able to solve simple problems such as Towers of Hanoi, but real-world problems were found to be intractable due to combinatorial explosion.

Aside
An intractable problem generally has an algorithm (brute force search) that provides a solution, but the algorithm is too inefficient to be

---

[1]For details on how the GPS worked, see Newell, A.; Shaw, J.C.; Simon, H.A. (1959). Report on a general problem-solving program. Proceedings of the International Conference on Information Processing. pp. 256–264.

practical due to the number of possibilities to be checked. Combinatorial explosion refers to the rapid growth in the number of possibilities as the problem size increases.

Consider a game of chess. White has 20 legal options for his first move, and so does black. Thus, there are 400 legal board states after each player has taken his first move; after the second set of moves, the total number of possibilities is into six figures.

When general-purpose problem solvers proved impractical, research moved more into single-purpose *expert systems*, where human experts in a particular area would explicitly encode their knowledge so that the expert system has a large knowledge base that its inference engine can apply to a given problem. This is useful in fields such as medicine[2] where a vast amount of relevant information can be applied to a problem; the system can make inferences that would otherwise require a human expert in the field.

A *subsymbolic* AI, rather than following rules, uses equations to arrive at its conclusions. Where symbolic AI uses rules devised by humans (and thus can display the reasoning it uses to reach its conclusion), subsymbolic AI "learns" to solve a problem without actually having defined rules for how to arrive at the solution. Subsymbolic AI is inspired by how neurons in our brains process information. A neuron receives input from other neurons that connect to it, and if the weighted sum[3] of those

---

[2]There have been a number of expert systems in the medical field, some more successful than others.

[3]Weighed sum means that not all inputs are counted equally;

inputs reaches a threshold, that neuron fires as well.

A subsymbolic AI can be assigned a random set of weights to apply to its inputs and then trained. If it gets the wrong answer, it adjusts those weights slightly to move it closer to the correct answer for that input. Over many examples, the values eventually reach a point where the AI can perform well on the task, even though it doesn't have an algorithm for what it does - only a collection of values. This brings us to machine learning, where an AI is able to learn from experience without being explicitly programmed to solve the task, with humans simply correcting the machine when it makes an error.

Practical example

In 2020, researchers at UC San Diego developed a machine learning algorithm to recognize COVID-19 in chest X-rays. The algorithm has successfully flagged cases of COVID-19 that were not caught by radiologists.

36.2   Subfields of AI

It is comparatively easy to make computers exhibit adult level performance on intelligence tests or playing checkers, and difficult or impossible to give them the skills of a one-year-old when it comes to perception and mobility.

- Hans Moravec, 1988

---

some connections are stronger than others and those inputs are given more weight.

Moravec's paradox is that computers are often very good at things that humans are bad at, but helpless at things that even a small child finds simple. The most challenging areas in artificial intelligence are often tasks for which humans have unconsious competence: recognizing faces, catching a ball, understanding language. Many of these problems have now spawned their own subfields of AI, some of which were mentioned above. They include (but are not limited to):

Computer vision
This field attempts to teach a computer to recognize objects in images or videos.

Natural language processing
This field is concerned with teaching computers to understand human language.

Neural networks and machine learning
A neural network is a set of algorithms used to recognize relationships. The network is used in machine learning.

Planning
The computer decides what actions to take to reach a desired goal.

Robotics
Robots must be able to navigate and respond to unexpected events in the real world.

Speech processing
This area includes both recognizing and generating speech.

Figure 36.1: A robot practicing computer vision.

36.3 Examples

AI has become common in everyday life. A few examples that many readers will be familiar with:

- Voice-activated assistants such as Siri and Alexa recognize and process speech.

- Spam filters learn to recognize spam while allowing legitimate email through, and adapt to changing spam techniques.

- Depositing a check from your phone requires being able to recognize letters and numbers from an image.

- Self-driving cars recognize and avoid obstacles in real time. A robot vacuum determines the best way to clean a room and return to its charger.

- Amazon predicts what items we might be interested in purchasing and shows them to us, even ensuring they'll be available when it thinks we might purchase.[4]

---

[4]In 2014, Amazon obtained a patent for anticipatory shipping, in which it ships products it thinks you're likely to buy to your local warehouse prior to you purchasing them. The company anticipates even shipping an item to you before you order it.

Chapter 37

Quantum Computing[1]

So far in this book, we have restricted ourselves to classical computers, although we mentioned quantum mechanics in Chapter 21.

> **Terminology**
>
> A *classical computer* is simply a computer that is not a quantum computer. It relies only on classical mechanics, while a quantum computer requires features of quantum mechanics.

A quantum computer uses quantum mechanical phenomena to compute probabilities. Rather than bits, we deal with qubits (quantum bits), which can represent multiple states at once. Given a problem, we calculate the probability of all possible answers, and select the answer that has the greatest probability of being correct.

---

[1]The technical editor for this book, who does research in quantum computing, contributed to this chapter.

37.1 Physics

Quantum physics deals with how things behave at the subatomic level. Several concepts will be important in quantum computing:

superposition
> This is the ability of a quantum system to be in more than one state at the same time. A qubit may be in a superposition of 0 and 1; it is both 0 and 1 (with some probability of each) until it is measured.

entanglement
> When two or more particles are entangled, the quantum state of each particle becomes correlated with that of the others. Measuring the state (spin, polarization, position, momentum) of one particle affects the others, even if they are separated by a great distance.[2]

quantum measurement
> When the state of a quantum system is measured, the quantum state collapses into a single classical state. Each qubit is now either a 0 or a 1, rather than existing in a superposition of states.

37.2 Theoretical considerations

Quantum computers don't actually solve different problems from classical computers; they can still be simulated

---

[2]Einstein called this behavior "spooky action at a distance".

by a Turing machine. What they can do is solve problems that would be impractical on a classical computer, because the best known algorithms require checking a vast number of possibilities.[3]

37.3 Practical considerations

Until recently, quantum computers were found only in the lab and provided only a handful of qubits, but they are now commercially available.[4] As of this writing, quantum computers are still used for research rather than for practical applications. However, the technology is improving quickly, and multiple quantum programming languages are ready to go.

---

[3]In 2019, Google used a 53-qubit quantum computer to solve a very particular problem in 200 seconds. The result was verified by the Summit supercomputer at Oak Ridge National Laboratory; IBM researchers estimated that under ideal conditions and with extra memory, Summit could accomplish the task in two and a half days.

[4]You can run quantum circuits on IBM's quantum computer at https://quantum-computing.ibm.com/ and use Leap's D-Wave 2000Q quantum computer at https://www.dwavesys.com/take-leap.

Afterword

You've reached the end of A Programmer's Guide to Computer Science!

Of course, we've only scratched the surface. Entire books could be (and have been) written about what we've discussed in each chapter. At this point, however, you've been exposed to the vast majority of topics you could expect to see in an undergraduate course on computer science, other than mathematics and other out-of-major areas. If there are topics you'd like to learn more about, you now have the background to know what to search for.

If you've enjoyed this book, reviews are greatly appreciated. If you have a question or comment about the material, feel free to reach out to me. You can contact me through my website at `http://www.whatwilliamsaid.com/books/`, where you can also sign up for my mailing list. I'm also on Twitter at @wmspringer.

I've been asked if there will be a Volume 3, and the answer is no; I've covered what I wanted to cover. That said, there will likely be more books in the programmer's guide series. As a deaf developer, I'm hoping to write a volume on accessibility. As a senior developer with nearly a decade of experience working on large, complex software, I'd like to write a book on professional software development for new programmers. After that, who knows?

Index